PRINCEWILL LAGANG

Militias, Mercenaries, and Minerals: The International Business of War in DR Congo

Contents

1

Introduction

T he Democratic Republic of the Congo (DRC) has long been a
country defined by crisis and conflict, much of which stems from its
abundant natural resources. The vast deposits of minerals such as
gold, diamonds, and cobalt have made the country a prime target for foreign
exploitation, but instead of prosperity, these resources have fueled a cycle
of violence. The constant battle for control of these valuable commodities
has led to widespread suffering, with local militias, mercenaries, and foreign
powers contributing to the chaos. The wealth of the country, instead of being
a blessing, has become a curse.

This book examines the complex relationship between war and business,
focusing on how the DRC's rich resources have become a central element
in the global economy—and a source of unrelenting violence. Militias and
mercenaries, often backed by both local and international actors, have used
the control of mineral-rich territories as a means to fund their operations
and further their agendas. Rather than bringing stability, the competition
for these resources has only intensified the conflict, leaving the Congolese

people to suffer the consequences.

A crucial aspect of this conflict is the involvement of foreign powers, multinational corporations, and private military contractors, all of whom have stakes in the DRC's mineral wealth. These external actors have played a significant role in shaping the conflict, at times fueling the violence to secure their economic interests. Through their actions, they have perpetuated a system where the pursuit of profit drives political and military strategies, deepening the suffering of local communities and prolonging the war.

In exploring the intersection of global business and local violence, this book reveals how the DRC's mineral wealth has become entangled with political and economic power struggles. The result is a devastating war economy, where both local and international actors exploit resources while disregarding the human toll. Understanding this dynamic is key to addressing the conflict, as it highlights the central role that global business interests play in keeping the DRC trapped in a cycle of war.

2

The DRC's Precious Resources

C hapter 1:

The Democratic Republic of the Congo (DRC) is one of the world's richest countries in terms of natural resources, boasting vast deposits of minerals that are critical to global industries. The country is a major source of cobalt, a vital component in the production of batteries for smartphones, electric cars, and other modern technologies. In addition to cobalt, the DRC is also rich in gold, diamonds, coltan, and other minerals that are highly sought after worldwide. These resources should theoretically lead to national prosperity, but instead, they have become a curse, contributing to the ongoing conflict and instability in the region. The DRC's wealth has attracted numerous foreign and local actors, all eager to capitalize on the riches beneath the country's soil, turning the region into a battleground.

The competition for control over these valuable resources has fueled both local and foreign-driven conflicts. Militias, foreign mercenaries, and multinational corporations have all sought to gain control of the DRC's mining areas and lucrative trade routes. Rather than leading to development, the presence of these actors has only deepened the violence and exploitation. These actors are motivated by the wealth that can be extracted from the land, with little regard for the human cost of their actions. The country's mineral resources have, therefore, become a central element in the war economy, where violence and greed are perpetuated in the pursuit of profit.

One of the most significant consequences of this struggle over resources is the rise of armed groups and militias, which fight for control of mines and transportation routes. These groups, often well-funded by external actors, have wreaked havoc on local communities, forcing civilians to work in unsafe, exploitative conditions. The resources intended to bring economic benefit have instead funded conflict, making the DRC's mineral wealth a double-edged sword. This chapter delves into how this cycle of exploitation and violence perpetuates the conflict, with no clear resolution in sight as long as external and local actors continue to vie for control over the country's riches.

Ultimately, the DRC's precious resources have been a major catalyst for the conflict, rather than a pathway to prosperity. The international community, along with regional powers, must grapple with the complicated relationship between wealth and violence in the DRC. As long as the demand for these resources continues to grow, and as long as local and foreign actors are willing to exploit them at the expense of human lives, the cycle of conflict and instability will persist. This chapter explores how the quest for resources has kept the DRC in a perpetual state of war, undermining efforts for peace and prosperity.

3

The Rise of Militias

C hapter 2:

Militias have become a defining feature of the conflict in the DRC, playing a crucial role in the struggle for control over the country's resources. These armed groups, often composed of local fighters, emerged as a response to the power vacuum created by the state's weakness and the influx of external actors. The militias claim to represent various interests, from ethnic groups and political factions to personal profit-seeking motives. Some argue they are fighting for the protection of their communities, while others are simply motivated by the control of mineral-rich areas. What began as local grievances quickly escalated into larger, more organized armed groups that are deeply entrenched in the DRC's war economy.

The rise of these militias is not solely a local phenomenon, however. Many of these groups have received backing from foreign powers, including neighboring countries like Rwanda and Uganda, as well as multinational corporations eager to secure control over valuable mineral resources. These foreign-backed militias often operate with impunity, using violence and intimidation to seize mining areas, and they are regularly involved in the illegal smuggling of minerals out of the country. While some militias represent legitimate political or ethnic aspirations, others are nothing more than violent proxies for external interests, perpetuating a cycle of exploitation and conflict that continues to devastate local populations.

Militias operate outside the law, making it nearly impossible for the Congolese government to regain control of vast swathes of its territory. These groups often loot, pillage, and exploit local communities, displacing civilians and subjecting them to violence. The lack of state presence and governance in these areas has created a fertile ground for these militias to thrive, further destabilizing an already fragile country. The DRC's government, corrupt and divided, has been unable to effectively address the militia problem, which has only fueled the ongoing violence and ensured that the country remains a battleground for competing factions.

The militias are often seen as both a cause and a symptom of the country's larger crisis. They contribute to the destabilization of the region by controlling mining areas and maintaining power through force. Their rise is a direct result of the DRC's weak state institutions and the influx of foreign interests, which have turned the conflict into a struggle for resources rather than a battle over political or ethnic rights. This chapter will explore how the rise of these militias has shaped the conflict, and how their actions are inextricably linked to both local and international dynamics.

4

Mercenaries and Private Military Companies

C hapter 3:

    The role of mercenaries and private military companies (PMCs) in the DRC has added another layer of complexity to the war economy. These private contractors provide military services to a wide range of actors, including foreign governments, multinational corporations, and even local militias. In the DRC, where the government has struggled to maintain control and stability, PMCs have become essential players in the conflict. They offer armed protection to mining operations, serve as private armies for political factions, and help maintain the status quo for those invested in the ongoing violence.

The presence of mercenaries in the DRC highlights the blurred lines between business and warfare. These companies, often motivated by financial gain, are not bound by the same legal or ethical standards as traditional military forces. Many of these firms operate in regions where the Congolese government has no presence, creating a situation where private armies maintain control over strategic areas. This chapter examines the motivations behind the proliferation of mercenaries in the DRC and the economic incentives that drive their involvement in the conflict. For these mercenaries, the war in the DRC is a business opportunity, where the chaos of conflict provides financial rewards through contracts, security services, and resource protection.

Private military companies often enter the DRC under the guise of providing security, but their presence can be seen as a way for foreign powers and corporations to indirectly engage in the conflict without the risks of direct involvement. These companies typically have access to advanced military equipment and experienced personnel, making them valuable assets for those seeking to protect their investments in mining operations. The presence of mercenaries exacerbates the violence, as they are often willing to use extreme measures to safeguard their clients' interests. The involvement of these private forces further complicates the efforts to bring peace to the region, as their interests are aligned with the continuation of conflict rather than its resolution.

Mercenaries and PMCs operate in the shadows of the conflict, often with little accountability. Their operations are frequently hidden from public view, and they are rarely held responsible for the consequences of their actions. In a country as unstable as the DRC, where local and international powers struggle to find common ground, PMCs are often free to exploit the chaos for their own gain. This chapter will explore how mercenaries and private military companies shape the course of the war in the DRC, and how their presence has made it even more difficult to imagine a path to peace and stability for the country.

5

Foreign Governments and Strategic Interests

C hapter 4:

Foreign governments have had a profound influence on the ongoing conflict in the Democratic Republic of the Congo (DRC), with many external powers pursuing their own strategic and economic interests in the region. Neighboring countries such as Rwanda and Uganda have been deeply involved, each seeking to advance its own agenda by supporting various militias and armed groups within the DRC. For Rwanda, the presence of Hutu militants and the fear of instability spilling over into its borders have led to military interventions, while Uganda has sought to control strategic areas rich in resources. These interventions, often conducted through proxies, have complicated efforts to resolve the conflict and have fueled further instability in the region.

Beyond the African nations directly involved, global powers such as the

United States, China, and various European countries have also had a hand
in shaping the DRC conflict. For the U.S., the focus has largely been on
countering terrorism and securing regional stability, but the country's support
for some regional powers has at times unintentionally exacerbated the
violence. China, on the other hand, has become a significant player in the
DRC's resource extraction economy, making strategic investments to secure
access to the country's wealth in minerals such as cobalt and coltan, which
are crucial for technology production. Meanwhile, European countries,
particularly Belgium, have historically maintained a presence in the region,
given their colonial past, but their involvement now often revolves around
maintaining economic and geopolitical leverage.

The international arms trade also plays a significant role in prolonging
the DRC conflict. Global powers have been complicit in supplying arms to
various factions, either directly or through intermediaries, further fueling
violence. The steady flow of weapons has allowed militias and foreign-
backed forces to maintain their control over key mining areas and trade
routes, perpetuating the cycle of violence. This chapter delves into how
foreign governments, through their support for militias, mercenaries, and
corporations, have used the DRC as a strategic chessboard to further their
own national interests, often at the expense of the Congolese people.

The involvement of foreign powers in the DRC conflict underscores the
complex nature of the war economy, where the intersection of global politics,
strategic interests, and resource exploitation continues to drive violence.
While some international players claim to work toward peace and stability,
their actions often serve to perpetuate the underlying dynamics of the conflict.
The geopolitical struggle for control over the DRC's resources shows how
external interests—whether political, economic, or military—have directly
impacted the country's ability to find a lasting resolution to its crisis.

6

Multinational Corporations and Resource Extraction

C hapter 5:

Multinational corporations (MNCs) have been central to the exploitation of the Democratic Republic of the Congo's (DRC) vast natural resources, and they have played an indirect yet significant role in the perpetuation of the country's conflict. These companies, primarily from Western and Asian countries, have been eager to access the DRC's mineral wealth, which includes cobalt, copper, gold, and diamonds. The high demand for these resources—critical to global industries like electronics, technology, and energy—has incentivized these corporations to overlook the devastating consequences their operations have on local communities. Through partnerships with local militias and foreign governments, MNCs have been able to extract resources while keeping a hands-off approach to the violence that often accompanies their operations.

In exchange for access to these valuable minerals, MNCs have at times provided funding or logistical support to militias controlling key mining territories. This relationship has been one of mutual benefit, as militias offer protection to mining operations and ensure the steady flow of minerals to international markets. Unfortunately, this often involves egregious human rights abuses, including forced labor, displacement, and violence against local populations. As MNCs profit from the DRC's resources, they rarely bear the full responsibility for the suffering caused by their operations, and their willingness to ignore the conditions under which the minerals are extracted allows the conflict to persist.

This chapter delves into the ethical dilemmas faced by multinational corporations operating in such a volatile and lawless environment. Many companies argue that they are simply following global demand and that their presence brings some form of economic benefit, such as employment and infrastructure development. However, these arguments often ignore the larger picture: that the conflict itself is being fueled by the resources being extracted and that the benefits rarely reach the local population. MNCs are often seen as profit-driven entities that prioritize resource extraction over the welfare of the Congolese people, contributing to the perpetuation of the DRC's war economy.

The global supply chains that rely on conflict minerals from the DRC create an international market for exploitation and violence. As long as the demand for minerals extracted in conflict zones remains high, corporations will continue to engage in business practices that support the status quo. This chapter also discusses the efforts by international organizations, such as the United Nations, to hold companies accountable for the role they play in the DRC conflict. While there have been some attempts to regulate supply chains and impose ethical sourcing guidelines, the challenge remains in enforcing these standards and ensuring that companies operate responsibly. Ultimately, MNCs play a crucial role in shaping the conflict by enabling the flow of resources that fund both the militias and the mercenaries involved in the DRC's war economy.

7

The Plight of Civilians

C hapter 6:

The people of the Democratic Republic of the Congo (DRC) have borne the brunt of the conflict that has raged for decades, suffering tremendous humanitarian consequences as various armed groups, mercenaries, and foreign corporations battle for control of the country's mineral wealth. Civilians in the DRC are caught in a brutal crossfire, forced to endure violence, displacement, and poverty as multiple factions vie for power. The country's war economy has made everyday life a struggle for survival, with entire communities uprooted and subjected to the whims of armed militias, who often see the local population as a means to an end in their pursuit of resources.

The humanitarian crisis in the DRC is dire. Millions have been displaced, both internally and across borders, as a result of the conflict. These displaced persons often find themselves in overcrowded refugee camps with little access to food, clean water, or medical care. The violence unleashed by armed groups and mercenaries leaves civilians vulnerable to atrocities such as sexual violence, abductions, and forced labor. Entire villages are wiped out in pursuit of mining areas or trade routes, and communities that once thrived are now ghost towns. Despite the massive scale of suffering, the international response has often been inadequate, with humanitarian organizations struggling to reach those in need due to the ongoing insecurity and lack of infrastructure.

The international community has attempted to address the crisis through peacekeeping missions, such as those led by the United Nations, and through humanitarian aid. However, these efforts are often hampered by the entrenched power structures in the region, as well as the complexity of the conflict. Peacekeepers face significant challenges in maintaining order, especially in areas controlled by militias and mercenaries, and aid agencies often find themselves at the mercy of armed groups who demand protection or payment in exchange for access to vulnerable populations. The result is that even well-meaning international efforts can fall short, leaving many civilians trapped in a perpetual state of suffering.

This chapter explores how the war economy has directly impacted the lives of the Congolese people, from the destruction of livelihoods to the breakdown of basic societal structures. It also highlights the resilience of the people who continue to survive amidst the violence, often relying on local networks of support to get by. While international aid and peacekeeping missions have played a role in alleviating some of the suffering, they have not been enough to address the root causes of the conflict. The plight of civilians remains one of the most tragic aspects of the war economy, as the DRC's resources continue to fuel the violence that devastates its people.

8

Corruption and Governance Failures

C hapter 7:

The Democratic Republic of the Congo (DRC) has long struggled with a system plagued by corruption and ineffective governance, which has deeply exacerbated the conflict and allowed external actors and armed groups to operate with impunity. The lack of a strong, functional government has created an environment where powerful figures, both within the country and abroad, can manipulate the situation for personal gain. Corrupt leaders have often turned a blind eye to the activities of militias and mercenaries, allowing them to profit from the country's rich natural resources without fear of reprisal. This failure in governance has meant that those in power rarely face any consequences, perpetuating a cycle of instability and hindering efforts to bring peace to the region.

The relationship between government officials and armed groups has often been symbiotic, with political elites benefiting from the chaos caused by militias, as it enables them to maintain control over resource-rich areas.

Many government officials have used their positions to profit from the war economy, either by directly participating in the exploitation of minerals or by accepting bribes from foreign companies and armed factions. The absence of accountability has created a culture of impunity, where even as the people of the DRC suffer, political leaders and warlords continue to enrich themselves. The lack of transparency in government activities and the pervasive corruption in key sectors, including security forces and mining industries, has made it difficult for the state to regain control of its territory.

This chapter also examines how the weak governance structure has allowed foreign powers, both governmental and corporate, to exploit the country's resources with little oversight or regulation. These external actors often work with corrupt officials or armed groups, further compounding the problems of the DRC. The inability of the Congolese government to assert control over its own territory has left a vacuum in which regional powers and multinational corporations can act freely, with no regard for the long-term stability of the country. The failure to establish a functional and legitimate government has been a major obstacle to peace and development in the DRC, as it leaves the country vulnerable to exploitation and manipulation from both domestic and foreign actors.

The chapter concludes by discussing how addressing the issue of corruption and governance is essential to any long-term solution for the DRC. Without systemic reform to reduce corruption and strengthen the rule of law, the government will continue to be unable to exercise control over its resources or territory. Only through establishing accountability, transparency, and political will can the DRC hope to break the cycle of exploitation and instability that has plagued it for decades. Effective governance is the foundation upon which lasting peace and development must be built.

9

The Role of International Aid and NGOs

C hapter 8:

International aid organizations and non-governmental organizations (NGOs) have played an essential role in providing
humanitarian assistance to the people of the Democratic Republic of the
Congo (DRC), particularly in conflict zones where local services have
collapsed. They provide critical resources such as food, medical care, and
shelter to displaced populations, many of whom live in dire conditions due
to the ongoing conflict. However, despite these efforts, the war economy
and the complex network of militias, mercenaries, and corrupt officials have
undermined the effectiveness of aid programs. In some cases, aid has been
misdirected or misused, exacerbating the very problems it aims to solve.

One of the primary challenges faced by international aid organizations in
the DRC is the difficulty in reaching those who need help the most. Armed
groups often control large areas of the country and frequently intercept

or redirect humanitarian shipments, either for their own use or to sell on the black market. In some instances, NGOs are forced to negotiate with these armed groups to gain access to certain regions, which can lead to compromises and even exploitation. Furthermore, corrupt government officials have sometimes diverted aid for personal gain, further undermining the effectiveness of relief efforts. This dynamic not only reduces the impact of humanitarian aid but also places aid workers in danger, as they become targets of armed groups seeking control over resources.

In addition to these operational challenges, international aid efforts in the DRC have often struggled to address the root causes of the conflict. While humanitarian assistance can alleviate immediate suffering, it does little to resolve the structural problems that fuel the violence, such as the exploitation of resources, political corruption, and the absence of strong governance. This chapter explores how the failure to integrate peacebuilding and development goals into humanitarian aid programs has limited their long-term effectiveness. Aid organizations, while providing essential support, have sometimes found themselves caught in the complex web of local power struggles, unable to bring about meaningful change in the underlying causes of the war.

Ultimately, the role of international aid and NGOs in the DRC is a double-edged sword. While their contributions have undoubtedly saved countless lives, their impact has been limited by the conflict's deep-rooted causes. The chapter concludes by calling for a more integrated approach to aid—one that not only addresses the immediate humanitarian needs but also works to create the conditions necessary for sustainable peace. This involves focusing on governance reform, community resilience, and local empowerment, alongside traditional relief efforts, to break the cycle of conflict and humanitarian dependence.

10

The Economics of War

C hapter 9:

The economics of war are central to the ongoing conflict in the Democratic Republic of the Congo (DRC), where violence and instability have become a way of life for many communities. The war economy is driven by the extraction and trade of the country's rich natural resources, including minerals such as gold, diamonds, and cobalt. These resources fuel the conflict, as militias, mercenaries, and foreign actors fight to control the lucrative mining areas and trade routes. In this chapter, we examine how the financial incentives created by the war have perpetuated violence, as various groups use economic means to fund their operations and maintain power.

One of the primary drivers of the war economy in the DRC is the illegal mining of minerals, which is often controlled by armed groups and militias. These groups profit from the extraction and sale of these minerals, which are smuggled across borders or sold on the black market. The revenue generated from this illicit trade allows armed factions to purchase weapons, hire mercenaries, and maintain their hold over territory. Multinational corporations are often complicit in this system, purchasing conflict minerals with little regard for the human suffering that accompanies their extraction. The immense financial rewards from the war economy have thus created a complex web of interests that keep the conflict alive, as those involved have little incentive to seek peace or stability.

Mercenaries and private military companies (PMCs) play a significant role in the DRC's war economy by providing military services to those willing to pay. These private contractors often serve the interests of foreign powers, multinational corporations, or local militias. They offer protection for mining operations, secure supply chains, and even engage in direct combat to help control valuable resource areas. The presence of these mercenaries introduces a further layer of complexity to the conflict, as they operate for profit rather than ideological reasons, and their loyalty is often tied to the highest bidder. The growing reliance on PMCs has made it even harder to bring the war to an end, as these forces do not have a stake in peace but rather in maintaining the conflict's economic benefits.

The chapter also explores the challenges of peacebuilding in such an environment. With economic interests so deeply tied to the continuation of violence, finding a path to peace becomes increasingly difficult. The financial incentives to perpetuate the conflict are immense, and until these economic drivers are addressed, efforts to end the war will likely be futile. This chapter calls for a multifaceted approach to peacebuilding, one that includes not only diplomatic and military efforts but also efforts to dismantle the war economy. By targeting the financial structures that sustain the conflict, such as the illegal mineral trade and the mercenary networks, it may be possible to undermine the very foundation of the war itself and create the conditions for lasting peace.

11

The International Community's Response

C hapter 10:

The international community has faced significant challenges in its attempts to address the ongoing crisis in the Democratic Republic of the Congo (DRC). Efforts have included peacekeeping missions, diplomatic interventions, and the imposition of sanctions on foreign actors who contribute to the violence and instability. The United Nations (UN) has deployed peacekeepers to the region, but these missions have often been criticized for being underfunded, understaffed, and unable to effectively protect civilians or bring about lasting peace. Regional organizations, such as the African Union (AU) and the International Conference on the Great Lakes Region (ICGLR), have also attempted to mediate peace talks and promote regional cooperation, but their efforts have often been hindered by the complex nature of the conflict and the involvement of external powers with competing interests.

Sanctions have been imposed on individuals and entities believed to be fueling the conflict, including militias and corporations engaged in the illegal mineral trade. However, the effectiveness of these sanctions has been limited, as many of the key actors involved in the war economy are shielded by powerful allies. For example, countries that benefit from the mineral trade or have strategic interests in the region often block or circumvent international efforts to impose meaningful pressure on the DRC's warring factions. As a result, while the international community has made some attempts to curb the violence, these measures have frequently proven ineffective, as they fail to address the underlying economic and geopolitical factors that perpetuate the conflict.

Furthermore, there has been a disconnect between the humanitarian efforts aimed at alleviating suffering and the international political interests that drive the conflict. International aid organizations often find themselves caught in the crossfire, unable to operate effectively in a volatile environment where political and military actors have entrenched interests. Diplomatically, the international community has failed to present a united front or a clear strategy for achieving peace, with countries pursuing their own agendas in the region. The chapter emphasizes that achieving lasting peace will require a more coordinated and comprehensive approach, one that not only addresses the immediate humanitarian needs but also tackles the geopolitical and economic forces that continue to fuel the violence.

In conclusion, the international community's response to the DRC crisis has been fragmented and, at times, ineffective. Despite the considerable resources dedicated to peacekeeping and diplomacy, the deep-rooted economic and political interests at play in the region have often thwarted meaningful progress. Moving forward, the international community must adopt a more holistic approach, which includes greater political will, more effective sanctions, and more coordinated diplomatic efforts to address the broader issues that contribute to the conflict.

12

Potential Pathways to Peace

C hapter 11:

While the situation in the DRC remains dire, there are potential pathways to peace that could help break the cycle of violence. One crucial aspect of peacebuilding is addressing the global mineral trade, which has been a primary driver of conflict. By regulating the extraction and trade of minerals, international actors can ensure that the wealth generated from these resources benefits the people of the DRC rather than fueling armed groups and foreign exploitation. This could involve creating transparent supply chains, holding corporations accountable for their role in the conflict, and establishing mechanisms to ensure that minerals are extracted responsibly and ethically. Greater international cooperation is needed to monitor and control the flow of conflict minerals, particularly through the use of certification programs and trade restrictions on illegal mineral exports.

Another key pathway to peace lies in the reform of the Congolese gov-

ernment itself. The DRC's weak governance and widespread corruption
have been major obstacles to peace and stability. Strengthening institutions,
promoting transparency, and combating corruption are vital to creating a
government that can manage the country's resources responsibly and serve
the needs of its citizens. International support for democratic reforms,
improved governance, and the establishment of the rule of law will be essential
for building a foundation for peace. Local communities must be empowered
to participate in decision-making processes, ensuring that governance
structures are inclusive and representative of the diverse populations within
the country.

Strengthening local governance is also critical to achieving lasting peace.
Empowering communities to take control of their own security and resource
management can reduce the reliance on armed groups and militias. Decen-
tralized power structures can help restore order in regions where central
government authority is weak, and local leaders can work to rebuild trust and
social cohesion within their communities. In addition, fostering economic
development and creating alternative livelihoods for people in conflict zones
will help break the cycle of violence. By improving access to education,
healthcare, and infrastructure, the DRC can reduce the appeal of joining
militias or participating in illicit activities.

In conclusion, while the path to peace in the DRC is fraught with challenges,
there are tangible solutions that could help end the conflict. Regulation of the
mineral trade, government reform, and strengthening local governance are
essential steps in creating a more stable and peaceful environment. However,
these efforts must be backed by international cooperation, political will, and
sustained support from both regional and global actors. Only by addressing
the root causes of the conflict can the DRC begin to heal and move toward a
more peaceful future.

13

Moving Forward: The Future of the DRC

C hapter 12:

The future of the DRC depends on addressing the root causes of its prolonged conflict, which include the exploitation of its resources, the role of foreign actors, and the weaknesses of its government. Without tackling these issues head-on, the country will continue to be caught in a cycle of violence, instability, and poverty. The exploitation of the DRC's vast natural resources by armed groups, foreign mercenaries, and multinational corporations must be brought under control, with better regulation and oversight ensuring that these resources are used to benefit the Congolese people rather than fueling further conflict. The international community must play a critical role in facilitating this process by implementing stricter controls on the trade of conflict minerals and holding corporations accountable for their involvement in the war economy.

Strengthening governance in the DRC is equally vital for its future. The

Congolese government must be able to exercise control over its territory and resources, providing security and basic services to its citizens. This requires tackling corruption, building stronger institutions, and ensuring that the rule of law is upheld. Without a functioning government that can provide for the needs of its people and protect their rights, the DRC will remain vulnerable to exploitation and conflict. Political stability is essential for economic development, and it is through this development that the country can begin to heal and build a more prosperous future.

Additionally, regional cooperation and integration will be important in ensuring long-term peace and stability in the DRC. The involvement of neighboring countries, such as Rwanda and Uganda, has been a significant factor in exacerbating the conflict. Therefore, fostering peaceful relations between these countries and ensuring that they respect the sovereignty of the DRC is essential for a stable future. This chapter calls for a renewed commitment to regional peacebuilding, with diplomatic and economic ties that encourage cooperation rather than competition over resources.

The prospects for a peaceful and stable future in the DRC remain uncertain, but with the right political will, international support, and reforms, the country can begin to break free from its cycle of violence. The future of the DRC lies in the hands of its people, and with the right leadership, governance, and external support, it is possible to reclaim control over its resources and build a more just and peaceful society. However, this will require sustained effort, international cooperation, and a commitment to addressing the underlying issues that have fueled the conflict for so long.

14

Conclusion

"Militias, Mercenaries, and Minerals" offers a sobering look at the complex and destructive relationship between the Democratic Republic of the Congo's (DRC) vast mineral wealth and the ongoing conflict that has plagued the country for decades. The DRC's natural resources, which should be a boon to its people, have instead become a driving force behind violence, exploitation, and instability. Multinational corporations, local militias, and foreign powers have all played a role in this exploitation, each seeking to profit from the country's mineral riches. The relentless competition for control over these resources has perpetuated a cycle of violence, where civilians bear the brunt of the suffering, and peace remains elusive.

The involvement of foreign governments and corporations has further complicated the situation. Rather than helping to stabilize the region, many international actors have contributed to the conflict by aligning themselves with armed groups or turning a blind eye to human rights abuses. These actors prioritize economic interests over the well-being of the Congolese people, making it difficult for meaningful peace to take hold. Meanwhile, local militias, often armed and financed by external forces, have continued to disrupt any efforts for lasting stability. This complex web of greed, power, and violence has kept the DRC trapped in a perpetual state of war.

However, the DRC's situation is not without hope. Despite the immense challenges, there is potential for the country to break free from its war economy. A concerted effort from both international and local leaders could shift the trajectory of the country toward peace and prosperity. This would require addressing the root causes of the conflict, particularly the relationship between resource exploitation and violence. By implementing stronger regulations on the global mineral trade, holding corporations accountable, and supporting local governance, the DRC could begin to untangle itself from the web of corruption and violence that has held it captive for so long.

Ultimately, the key to ending the DRC's suffering lies in the intersection of business and conflict. The country's wealth in natural resources need not be a curse if it is managed transparently and responsibly. With the right political will, international cooperation, and reforms to both governance and the mineral trade, the DRC has the potential to transform its situation. Only then can the people of the DRC hope to fully benefit from their country's riches, leading to a future of peace, stability, and prosperity for all.

www.ingramcontent.com/pod-product-compliance
Ingram Content Group UK Ltd.
Pitfield, Milton Keynes, MK11 3LW, UK
UKHW022005140225
455059UK00011B/370